Different but Special

By Owen Rex Daughtry   Edited by Janie M. Best

Illustrations by Susan Shorter

AuthorHouse™
1663 Liberty Drive
Bloomington, IN 47403
www.authorhouse.com
Phone: 833-262-8899

Because of the dynamic nature of the Internet, any web addresses or links contained in this book may have changed since publication and may no longer be valid. The views expressed in this work are solely those of the author and do not necessarily reflect the views of the publisher, and the publisher hereby disclaims any responsibility for them.

Any people depicted in stock imagery provided by Getty Images are models, and such images are being used for illustrative purposes only.
Certain stock imagery © Getty Images.

This book is printed on acid-free paper.

ISBN: 978-1-4520-8593-7 (sc)

Library of Congress Control Number: 2010914652

Print information available on the last page.

Published by AuthorHouse 01/13/2022

authorHOUSE®

To other kids like me with disabilities

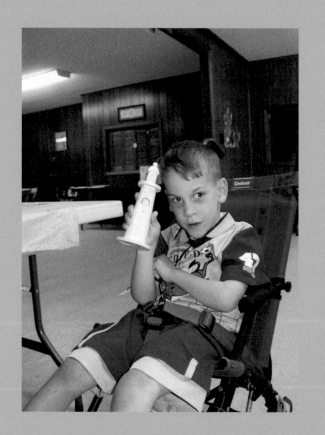

Hi! My name is Owen Rex Daughtry and I'm different! I am a smart little boy just like other kids, but I have cerebral palsy. Like other kids, I enjoy playing video games, watching TV, and working on my computer. I even joined the Boy Scouts for several years. It was fun to make crafts, earn merit badges, and sell popcorn to family and friends. I was a popcorn salesman for many years and earned scholarship money.

Cerebral palsy is a medical condition that keeps children from running and playing like other kids. It means that I cannot play sports like my brothers because I cannot hit a baseball or throw a basketball. I have limited use of my left arm and hand. The left side of my body, including my left arm, is weak because the left side of my brain suffered lack of oxygen when I was born.

I cannot walk or run like many of you, but I'm never going to give up. I take physical therapy twice a week to strengthen my muscles in hopes that one day I will walk!

Russ is my older brother and he loves to play baseball.

Michael is my younger brother and he loves basketball.

I'm SAD because I can't play ball and run with them, but I still love them very much. We do have fun playing video games together, and sometimes we play catch. They throw a ball to me in my wheelchair, and I throw it back to them. Throwing a ball helps me to exercise my arms and make them strong.

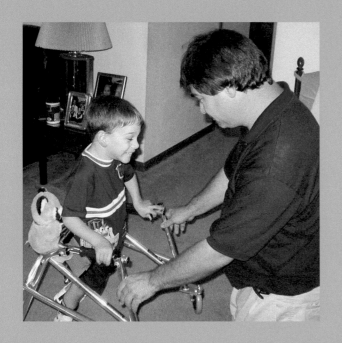

Will I ever be able to run and play? I sometimes wonder what it would be like to get out of this wheelchair and run a race.

Maybe if I work hard in physical therapy, one day I'll be able to do everything that normal kids do. It would be fun to go to the park to run and play. I see other kids playing dodge ball and it looks like fun.

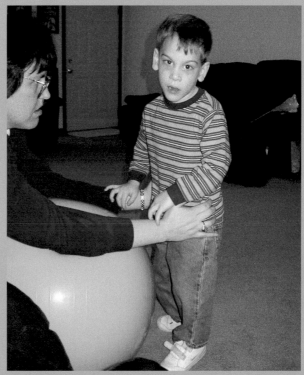

I remember my first day of preschool.

My mom woke me up early so I wouldn't be late. I was happy to be going to school but afraid of what people would think of me.

Mom dressed me in my favorite T-shirt and shorts. I wore my best tennis shoes that first day.

As my mom drove me to school, I sat looking out the window with a million questions running through my mind. Would my teacher like me? Would other boys and girls like me? Would other kids laugh at me?

Mom stopped at the Brogden Grill and bought me a biscuit before school. It was so good! The Brogden Grill was inside a gas station located a few miles from where we lived. It was a great place to pick up a quick breakfast before school in the morning.

Everything was perfect because I was finally going to school. All the big kids went to school, and I wanted to be grown up like them. But I wasn't like them; I was in a stroller, and Mom had to push me into the building.

I knew that Mom loved me, and she always told me that God made me **SPECIAL**, so I tried to be strong and decided not to be afraid.

Mom pushed me through the doorway at Selma School. The first thing I noticed was that the school building was very large. There were grownups everywhere as they hurried about their day.

My teacher, Mrs. Newsome, came up and welcomed me. She was so pretty and very nice. I knew that I would like being in her classroom.

WOW!

To my surprise, there were other kids in my classroom just like ME!

This might be fun after all!

I didn't feel so alone or even out of place here, because there were some other children who had special needs just like me. There was a boy in a wheelchair who could not talk well. It was hard to understand him.

Cassie was another new friend who used sign language to talk.
I had never seen that before! I soon learned to talk to Cassie using
my hands. How cool was that! Now I feel lucky because I *can* talk.
God made all of us SPECIAL ... but we are all different.

Mrs. Newsome needed lots of help with all of us, so she had a great assistant named Mrs. Creech.

At naptime, I slept on a cot. After naptime, we usually went home. We did not have to stay all day and we did not have very much homework because it was only preschool.

Once I learned that being different made me **SPECIAL** and could also be **FUN**, I was much happier!

I was very outgoing and loved to talk, so at preschool, I was invited to lead the school in the Pledge of Allegiance. It was fun to be chosen for important jobs at school and church.

I was such a charmer that all the teachers and assistants loved me.

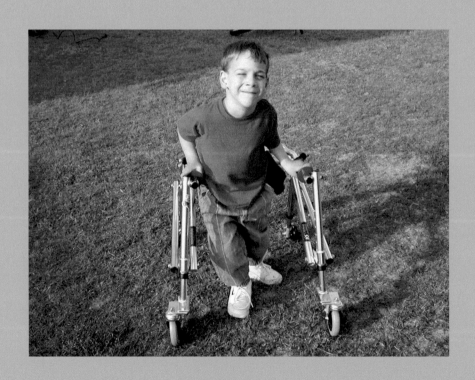

Some of the most fun I had was at the Special Olympics. My parents took me, and it was a great day for disabled children.

I was able to compete in games and win medals, which made my family VERY PROUD!

I made an acceptance speech, and all my family clapped for me. My mom took lots of pictures of me with all my medals. My parents rewarded my efforts by taking me out to lunch afterwards. It was a fun treat!

I won a medal in the walking competition. I used my walker in the competition, and my dad was there to keep me from falling. I never could walk by myself, but this was the next best thing.

Although throwing a tennis ball wasn't quite the same as throwing a football or baseball, I did my best and won a medal in that competition as well.

My grandparents went to see me compete in the games and were so proud of me! They were clapping their hands and cheering for me

the entire time. When I won a medal, their faces were beaming with pride and a smile as big as the sun. They were always there for me at every competition regardless of the weather. I could always count on them.

I have learned that there are SPECIAL programs for SPECIAL kids and that is why I have written this book. I want all kids who are handicapped to know they are SPECIAL and LOVED!

There are so many activities that children in a wheelchair can do if they just try and believe in themselves. Parents can find many resources at their local library to help their children in need.

You see …

Just because I cannot walk and run, it doesn't mean that I am broken. I have a heart of GOLD and I am very bright!

God gave me a good mind with a strong sense of will to do good and a sensitive heart. I always try hard to help others who are less fortunate, and I always try to be kind to everyone.

I have a keen sense of sight and hearing and often notice small details that others do not see. I often compliment my mom on a new dress or hairstyle when no one else has even noticed.

I have learned that having cerebral palsy does not mean I can't have a good life.

Yes, life is different, but I have learned to accept and live my life to the fullest with all its daily challenges.

I try not to feel sorry for myself, but sometimes it is very hard. When I feel sad, I think of others who are worse off than me. Then I am thankful—thankful to be with a loving family and friends. That makes me happy!

I'm truly thankful just to be ME!

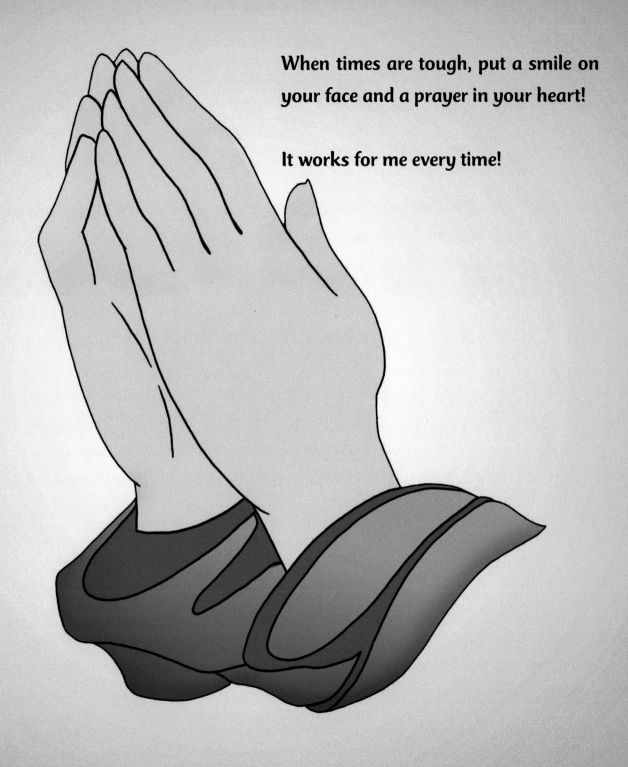

When times are tough, put a smile on your face and a prayer in your heart!

It works for me every time!

To all of you kids who are DIFFERENT, never forget how very SPECIAL you are to me, and ...

NEVER GIVE UP!

This book is dedicated to ALL of YOU,
and I hope it helps you understand *your*
special needs.

You can be ANYTHING you want to be if
you work hard and never give up!

Printed in the United States
by Baker & Taylor Publisher Services